NOËL! 2

CAROLS AND ANTHEMS
FOR ADVENT, CHRISTMAS & EPIPHANY
FOR MIXED VOICE CHOIRS

Selected & edited by David Hill

ISBN 978-1-84938-292-2

NOVELLO
part of **WiseMusic***Group*

EXCLUSIVELY DISTRIBUTED BY

Visit Hal Leonard Online at
www.halleonard.com

World headquarters, contact:
Hal Leonard
7777 West Bluemound Road
Milwaukee, WI 53213
Email: info@halleonard.com

In Europe, contact:
Hal Leonard Europe Limited
1 Red Place
London, W1K 6PL
Email: info@halleonardeurope.com

In Australia, contact:
Hal Leonard Australia Pty. Ltd.
4 Lentara Court
Cheltenham, Victoria, 3192 Australia
Email: info@halleonard.com.au

Introduction

Noël! 2 has been compiled to reflect the increasing demands for further choral material for the season of Advent, Christmas and Epiphany. The collection book includes familiar carols and anthems alongside a diverse range of new carol settings and hymns with original descants, all offering an extensive choice of styles to reflect the demands of mixed voice choirs with varying abilities and programming demands.

Timeless pieces have been included in order to provide a comprehensive selection of traditional repertoire (*In dulci jubilo*; *Hark! the herald angels sing*; *Once in royal David's city*; *O come, all ye faithful*; *Torches* and more), in conjunction with new arrangements of well loved classics (including *Coventry Carol*; *The first Nowell*; *Resonet in laudibus*; *Riu, riu, chiu* and *Silent night*). The version in this book of Peter Warlock's *Bethlehem Down* is an amalgamation of his arrangement for solo voice and piano (verses 1 and 3) with his famous four-part choral version (verses 2 and 4). My task was to dove-tail the two versions; every note is Warlock's. Additionally, there are several well known and unfamiliar works from core composers of the twentieth century (Herbert Howells; Gustav Holst; Kenneth Leighton) and there are several new carols from today's composers, to provide variety and fresh challenges (Richard Allain; Kenneth Hesketh; Richard Lloyd; Matthew Martin; John Tavener; Eric Whitacre and others).

Noël! 2 also includes the *'O' Antiphons* for use in Advent, transcribed from the *Cistercian Antiphonale*, which differ from other more frequently sung versions. The late Dr Mary Berry introduced them to me whilst I was at St John's College, Cambridge researching material for a recording of Advent and Christmas music.

The contents encompass works from all corners of the world and it is hoped that, whilst it is a reflection of modern trends in choral music, it also remains accessible to both amateur and professional singers.

Throughout the book I have suggested metronome and dynamic markings, these are marked in brackets and merely guidelines.

I am enormously grateful to my colleagues at Novello for their input, advice and expertise; in particular to Rachel Lindley, Kate Johnson, James Eggleston, Liz Robinson and also to Adrian Peacock.

David Hill
Cambridge, September 2009

Contents

A CD recording containing a selection of the music in this volume is available on
The Gift of Music® label (www.thegiftofmusic.com) recorded by Ikon
with David Dunnett (organ), directed by David Hill.

FRONT COVER *Nativity* (c.1913-14, painted limestone) by Eric Gill (1882-1940)
by kind permission of The Eric Gill Estate and the Bridgeman Art Library

BACK COVER photograph of David Hill by Paul Troughton

MUSIC SETTING Paul Ewers Music Design, Robin Hagues and John Mortimer
PROJECT MANAGEMENT Rachel Lindley

Order No. NOV310827
ISBN 978-1-84938-292-2

First performed by the Choir of Westminster Cathedral at St George's, Hanover Square, London
on December 19th 2006

Adam lay y-bounden

Words anon. 15th century

Matthew Martin

6

* Pronunciation: *finden* as in *Finland, taken* as in *tackle*

* Crescendo only on the lower note.

For the Chapel Choir of The King's School, Canterbury

Angelus ad Virginem

14th century carol
arr. Barry Rose

* *The rit. markings in Verses 1 & 2 may be omitted at the conductor's discretion.*

12

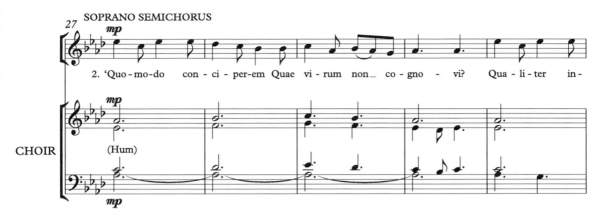

13

14

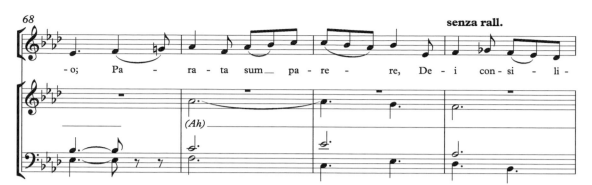

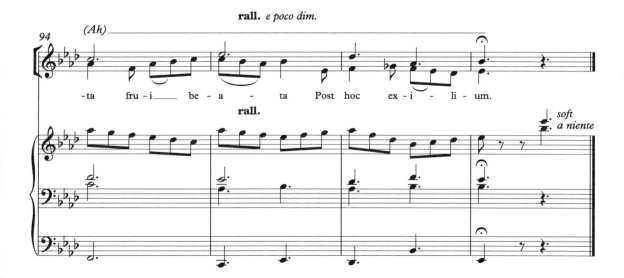

To Alice and Susannah

Away in a manger

William J. Kirkpatrick
arr. David Hill

stars in the__ bright sky looked down where he lay, The__ lit - tle Lord

(mm) _____ mm _____

(mm) _____ , mm ____

Je - sus, a - sleep on the hay.

(mm) _____

(mm) _____

mp

The__ cat - tle are__ low - ing, the__ Ba - by a - wakes,__ But__

mp

mp

lit - tle Lord Je - sus, no__ cry - ing he makes. I__ love__ thee, Lord

Je - sus! look__ down from the__ sky, And__ stay by__ my side un - til__

(Children or semichorus) *mp*

Be

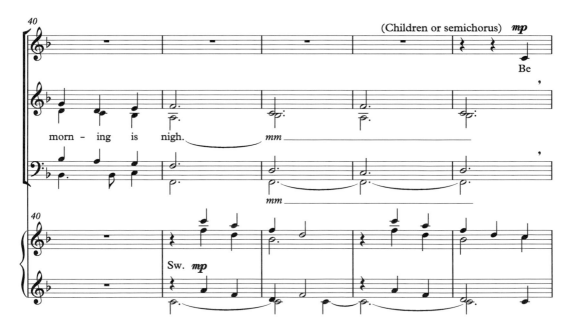

morn - ing is nigh.__ *mm*

mm

Sw. *mp*

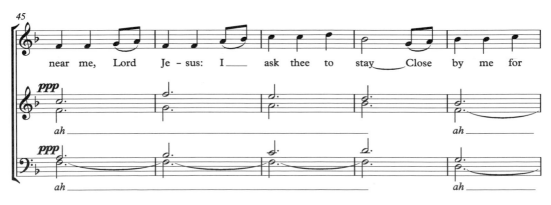

near me, Lord Je - sus: I__ ask thee to stay__ Close by me for

ppp

ah

ppp

ah

e - ver, and_ love me, I pray; Bless all the dear_ chil - dren in_

(ah) _____ ah _____

(ah) _____ ah _____

thy ten - der care, And_ fit us for hea - ven to_ live with thee

(ah) _____ ah _____

(ah) _____ ah _____

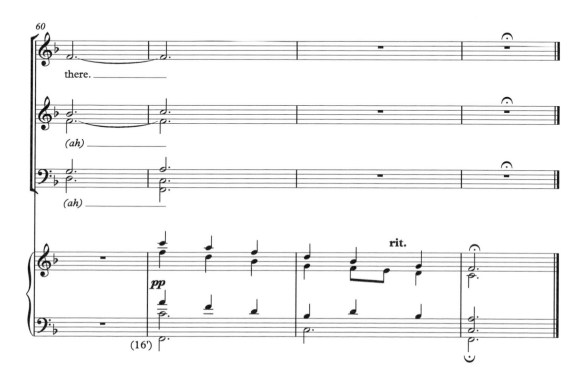

there. _____

(ah) _____

(ah) _____

rit.

pp

(16')

Bethlehem Down

Poem by Bruce Blunt

Peter Warlock
arr. David Hill

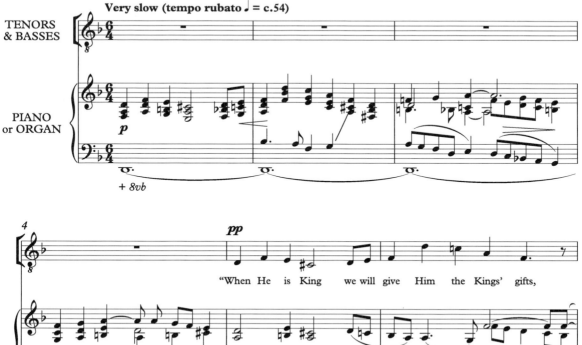

22

Sleep - ing so light - ly on Beth - le - hem Down.

Gt (solo)

cresc.

Here He has peace and a short while for dream-ing, Close hud - dled ox - en to

Here He has peace and a short while for dream - ing, Close hud - dled ox - en to

Here He has peace and a short while for dream - ing, Close hud - dled ox - en to

Here He has peace and a short while for dream - ing, Close hud - dled ox - en to

(for rehearsal only)

The Christ-child lay*

G.K. Chesterton
(1874-1936)

Kenneth Leighton

*Taken from Kenneth Leighton's *The World's Desire*, a Sequence for Epiphany

For Mike Brewer and Laudibus

Coventry Carol

arr. Richard Allain

Performance note: This carol may also be performed down a semitone.

TUTTI

38

The first Nowell

English traditional
arr. James O'Donnell

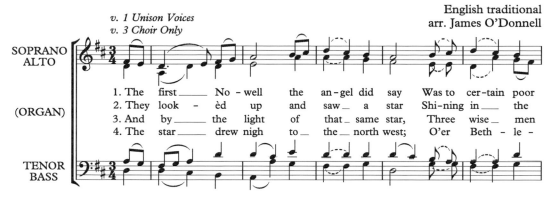

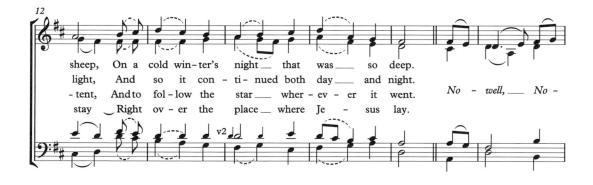

As an introduction, the Refrain should be used.

42

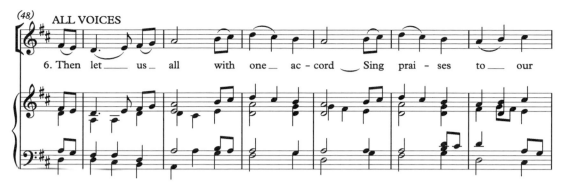

ALL VOICES

6. Then let___ us__ all with one__ ac-cord___ Sing prai-ses to___ our

heav'n-ly Lord, Who hath___ made heaven and earth___ of nought, And

with__ his blood__ man-kind__ hath bought. *No - well,___ No - well, No -*

-well, No - well: Born is the King___ of Is - ra - el.

Allarg.

To Nick Hill and the Chapel Choir of the Blue Coat School, Birmingham

Ding dong! merrily on high

Words by
G.R. Woodward

16th century French tune
arr. Stuart Nicholson

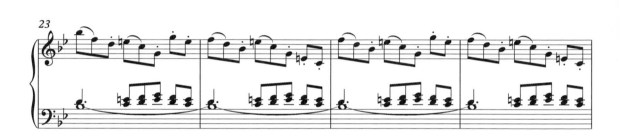

E'en so here be-low, be-low, let stee-ple bells be swung - en, __

E'en so here be-low, be-low, let stee-ple bells be swung - en, __

And i-o, i-o, i - o, by priest, peo - ple sung, by priest and peo-ple sung-en

And i-o, i-o, i - o, by priest, peo - ple sung, by priest and peo-ple sung-en

And i-o, i-o, i - o, by priest and peo-ple sung - en.

(*add pedal 16'*)

Pray you, du-ti-ful-ly prime your ma-tin chime, ye ring-ers;

May you beau-ti-ful-ly rime your eve-time song, ye sing-ers.

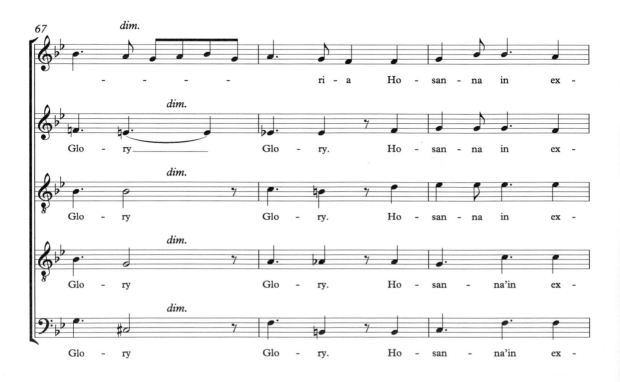

54

-cel - sis!

-cel - sis!

-cel - sis!

-cel - sis!

-cel - sis!

solo reed

Gt. mix &
pedal principal

senza rit.

(Tutti)

Gt.

solo

(add Ped. reed)

To John

E'en so, Lord Jesus, quickly come

Revelation 22
adapted by Ruth Manz

Paul Manz

and shed his blood That we might sav - ed be.

and shed his blood That we might sav - ed be.

and shed his blood That we might sav - ed be. Sing

and shed his blood That we might sav - ed be. Sing

Sing ho - ly, ho - ly to our Lord, The Lord, Al - might - y

Sing ho - ly, ho - ly to our Lord, The Lord, Al - might - y

ho - ly, ho - ly to our Lord, The Lord, Al - might - y

ho - ly, ho - ly to our Lord, The Lord, Al - might - y

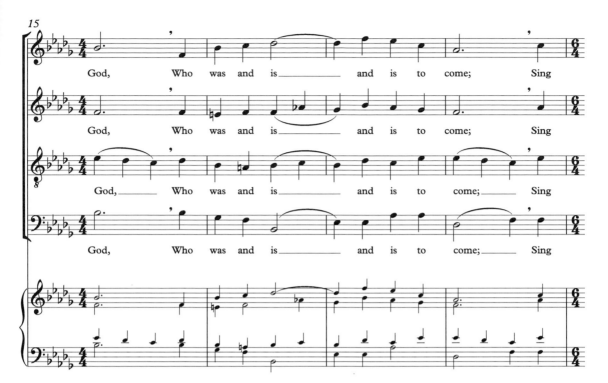

poco accel.

60

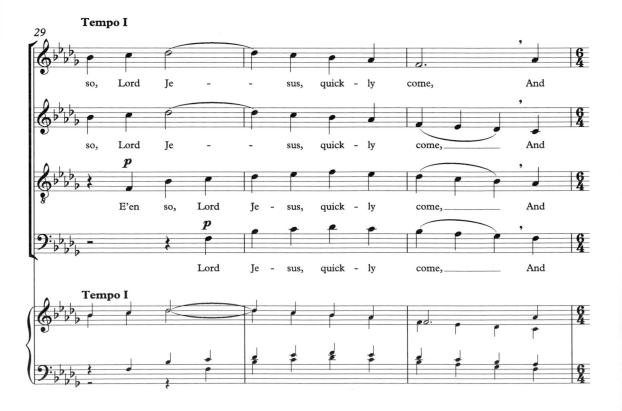

To Professor Ian Tracey

Gallery Carol

Anon.

Kenneth Hesketh

Lyrics:

1. Re - joice____ and be mer - ry in songs____ and in mirth,____ O praise____ our re - deem - er all mor - tals on earth.____ For this is the____ birth - day of Je - sus our

King,— who brought us sal - va - tion, His prai - ses we'll sing._____

2. A hea - ven - ly vi - sion ap - peared_ in the sky_____ vast num-bers of

ALTO

Ah,_____ Ah,_____

TENOR

Ah,_____ Ah,_____

BASS

Ah,_____ Ah,_____

64

prai - ses we'll sing.

3. Like

wise a bright star in the sky___ did ap - pear___ which led the wise

men from the East to draw near.___

4. And when they were come they their trea - sures un - fold,_____ and

un - to Him off - ered Myrrh, In - cense and Gold._____ So

(con 8ve bassa ad lib.)

For The Bach Choir

Gaudete!

14th century carol
arr. David Hill

Rejoice! Rejoice! Christ is born of the Virgin Mary: Rejoice!

Performance note: The verses can be sung by solo voices or a small group within each section.

1. *The time of grace has come for which we have prayed: let us devoutly sing songs of joy.*
2. *God is made man, while nature wonders; the world is renewed by Christ the King.*

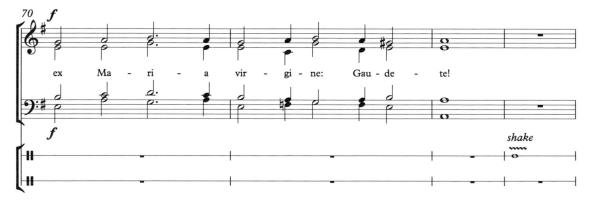

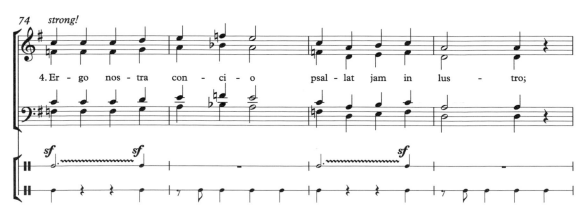

3. *The closed gate of Ezekiel has been passed through; from where the light has risen [The East] salvation is found.*
4. *Therefore let our assembly sing praises now at this time of purification: let us bless the Lord; greetings to the King.*

Gloria, sei dir gesungen

(Chorale from Cantata No.140 Wachet auf, ruft uns die Stimme)

J. S. Bach

Performance note: This could also be performed unaccompanied.

1. "Gloria" sing all our voices, with Angels all mankind rejoices, with harp and string in sweetest tone.
2. Twelve bright pearls adorn Thy Portals, where Thou hast gathered Thine Immortals as Angels round Thy glorious Throne.

No eye has ever seen, no ear has ever heard the joy we know. Our praises flow, I-o, I-o, to God in dulci jubilo!

Hark! the herald angels sing

C. Wesley, G. Whitefield,
M. Madan and others

Mendelssohn
Descant and organ part by
Christopher Robinson

DESCANT

3. Hail the heav'n - born Prince of Peace,___ Hail the Son___ of___

ALL OTHER VOICES

3. Hail the heav'n - born Prince of Peace!___ Hail the Son of

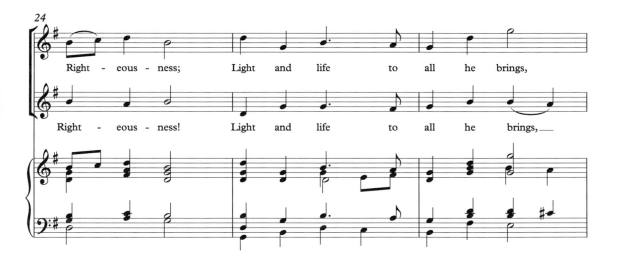

Right - eous - ness; Light and life to all he brings,

Right - eous - ness! Light and life to all he brings,___

Risen with heal - ing in___ his wings; Mild, he___ lays___ his___

Risen with heal - ing in his wings; Mild he lays his

glo - ry by, born that man no more may die;

glo - ry by, born that man no more may die;

born to raise the Sons of earth, born to give them se - cond birth:

born to raise the Sons of earth born to give them se - cond birth:

Hark! the he - rald an - gels sing glo - ry to the new-born King.

Hark! the he - rald an - gels sing glo - ry to the new-born King.

Hodie Christus natus est

Jan Pieterszoon Sweelinck

* the tempo relationship of ○ = ○. should continue at every change between duple and triple metre.

-li, No - e, No - e, No - e, No - e, No - e, No - e, No - e, No - e, No - e.

-li, No - e, No - e, No - e, No - e, No - e, No - e, No - e, No - e.

No - e, No - e, No - e, No - e, No - e, No - e.

No - e, No - e, No - e, No - e, No - e, No - e, No - e, No - e, No - e.

-li, No - e, No - e, No - e, No - e, No - e, No - e, No - e, No - e.

Ho - di - e, Ho - di - e ex - sul - tant ju sti, ex - sul - tant

Ho - di - e, Ho - di - e ex - sul - tant ju sti, ex - sul - tant

Ho - di - e, Ho - di - e ex - sul - tant ju sti, ex - sul - tant

Ho - di - e, ho - di - e ex - sul - tant ju - sti, ex - sul - tant

Ho - di - e, ho - di - e ex - sul - tant

88

Lullay my liking

Words from a "Mediaeval Anthology"

Gustav Holst

*Verses should be sung with flexibility whilst always mindful of the basic tempo.

REFRAIN

Lul-lay my lik-ing, my dear Son, my Sweet-ing; Lul-ly my dear Heart, mine own dear Dar-ling.

SOLO (3rd Verse)

There was mic-kle me-lo-dy At that child-és birth: Though the

song-sters were hea-ven-ly They mad-é mic-kle mirth.

REFRAIN

Lul-lay my lik-ing, my dear Son, my Sweet-ing; Lul-ly my dear Heart, mine own dear Dar-ling.

CHORUS (4th Verse)

An-gels bright they sang that night And said-en to that Child "Bless-ed be

Thou and so be she That is so meek and mild."

REFRAIN

Lul-lay my lik-ing, my dear Son, my Sweet-ing; Lul-ly my dear Heart, mine own dear Dar-ling.

SOLO (5th Verse)

Pray we now to that Child, As to His Mo-ther dear, God

grant them all His bless-ing That now ma-ken cheer.

REFRAIN

Lul-lay my lik-ing, my dear Son, my Sweet-ing; Lul-ly my dear Heart, mine own dear Dar-ling.

I wonder as I wander

John Jacob Niles

John Jacob Niles
arr. Kevin Grafton

peo - ple like you and like I... I won - der as I

wan - der out___ un - der the sky. When

FULL CHOIR *p*

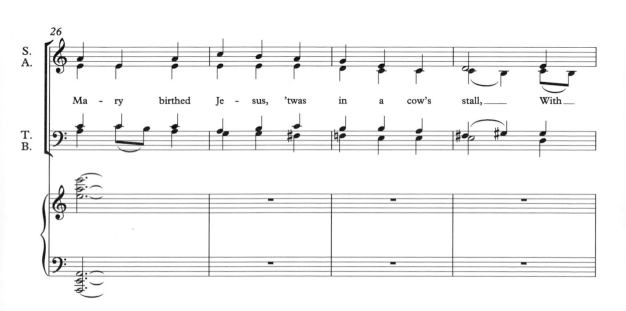

S.
A.

Ma - ry birthed Je - sus, 'twas in a cow's stall,___ With___

T.
B.

wise men and__ far - mers and shep - herds__ and__ all. But

high from the hea - vens__ a star's light did fall,_____ and the

pro - mise of a - ges it__ then did re - call.

he was___ the___ King.___

he was the King.

he was___ the___ King.___

he was the King.

subito *p*

pp

UNISON VOICES

p

Basses tacet

I won-der as I wan-der, out un-der the sky, How

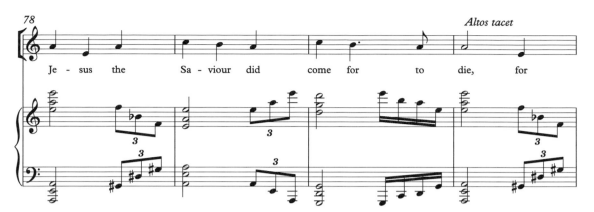

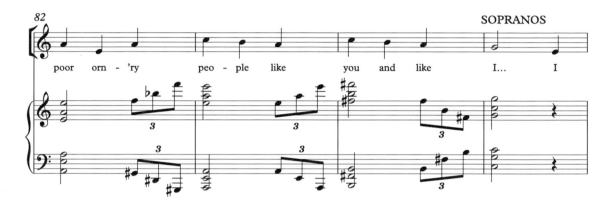

* i.e sing on an 'u' sound as in 'under'.

*For Jonathan Manners and DeChorum, on the occasion of the Cancer Research UK Carol Service at
All Saints Church, Weston-super-Mare on 22nd December 2008*

I wonder as I wander

John Jacob Niles

Richard Rodney Bennett

104

In dulci jubilo

Robert Pearsall

110

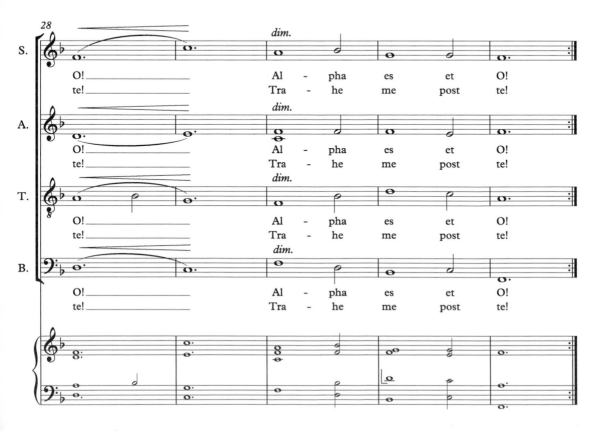

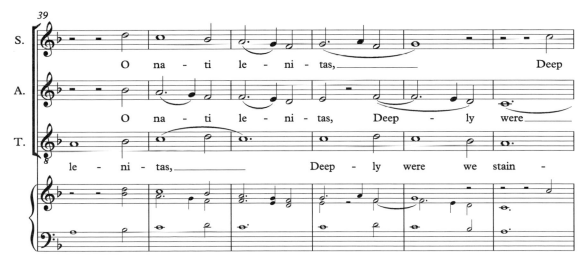

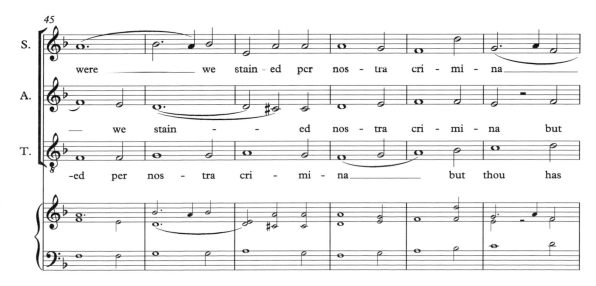

* as far as bar 64

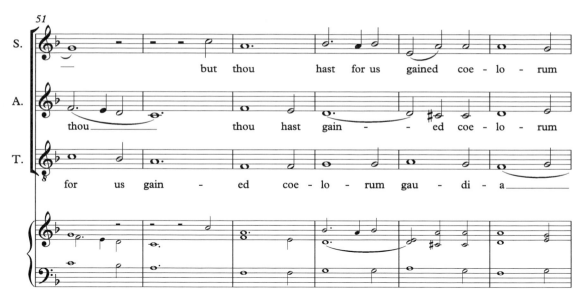

114

116

* In the original manuscript, the Alto note in bar 98 shows a D.

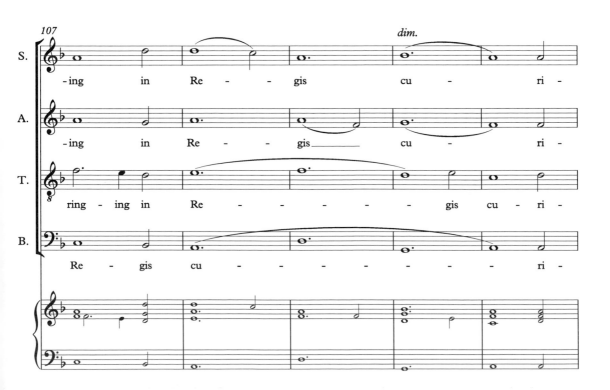

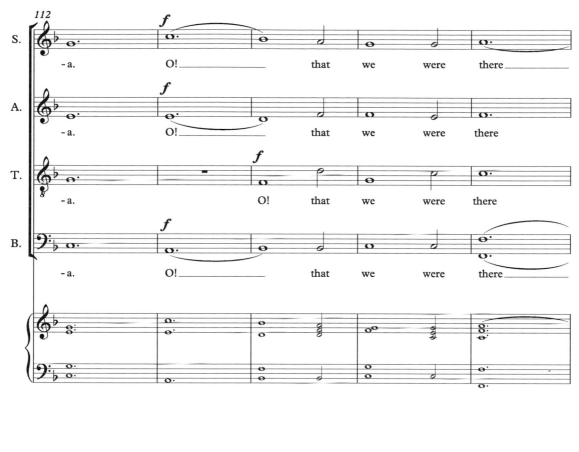

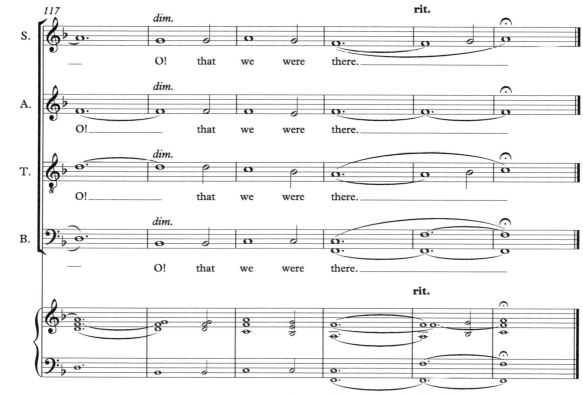

Jesus Christ the apple tree

New Hampshire, 1784

Elizabeth Poston
(1905–87)

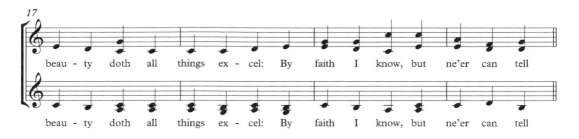

beau - ty doth all things ex - cel: By faith I know, but ne'er can tell

beau - ty doth all things ex - cel: By faith I know, but ne'er can tell

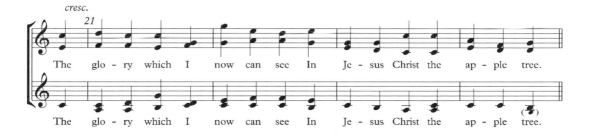

cresc.

The glo - ry which I now can see In Je - sus Christ the ap - ple tree.

The glo - ry which I now can see In Je - sus Christ the ap - ple tree.

4 PART or UNISON accompanied

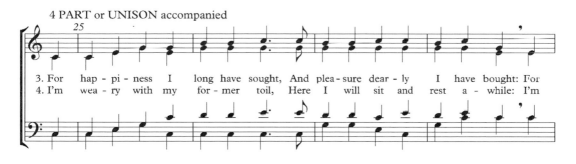

3. For hap - pi - ness I long have sought, And plea - sure dear - ly I have bought: For
4. I'm wea - ry with my for - mer toil, Here I will sit and rest a - while: I'm

hap - pi - ness I long have sought, And plea - sure dear - ly I have bought: I
wea - ry with my for - mer toil, Here I will sit and rest a - while: Un -

optional ending last time accompaniment only

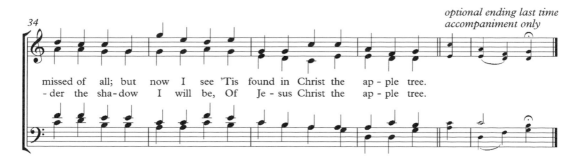

missed of all; but now I see 'Tis found in Christ the ap - ple tree.
- der the sha - dow I will be, Of Je - sus Christ the ap - ple tree.

To The Lady Margaret Singers, Cambridge

Long, long ago

John Buxton*

Herbert Howells

130

Love came down at Christmas

Christina Rossetti (1830-1894)

Richard Lloyd

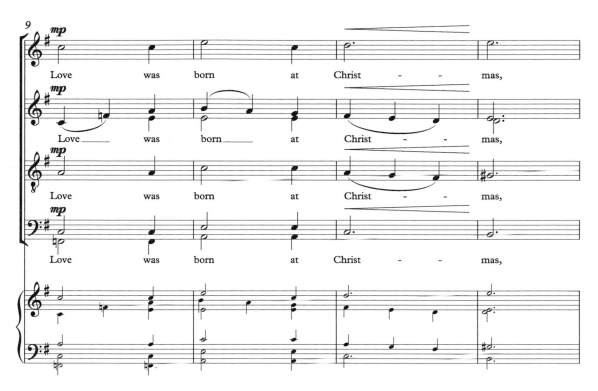

Love was born at Christ - - mas,
Love was born at Christ - - mas,
Love was born at Christ - - mas,
Love was born at Christ - - mas,

poco rit.

Star and an - gels gave the sign.
Star and an - gels gave the sign.
Star and an - gels gave the sign.
Star and an - gels gave the sign.

134

a tempo

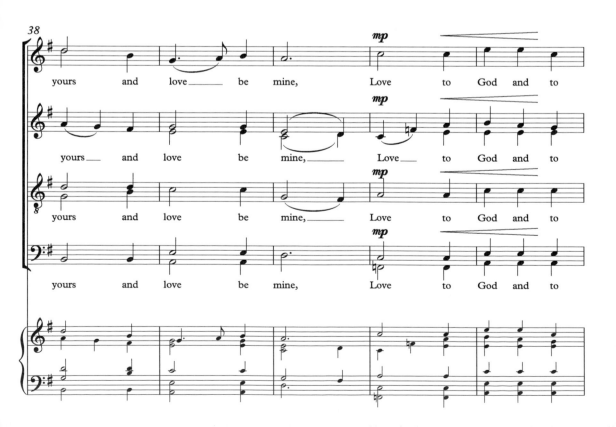

Lasset uns frohlocken
(No.5 of *Sechs Sprüche*, Op. 79)

Felix Mendelssohn-Bartholdy

Let our hearts be joyful,

140

the Saviour approacheth

whom God has proclaimed.

142

The name of the Lord shall be praised for evermore,

144

Alleluia!

Commissioned by the Master Chorals of Tampa Bay
for Dr. Jo-Michael Schiebe

Lux Aurumque

Edward Esch
Latin translation by
Charles Anthony Silvestri

Eric Whitacre

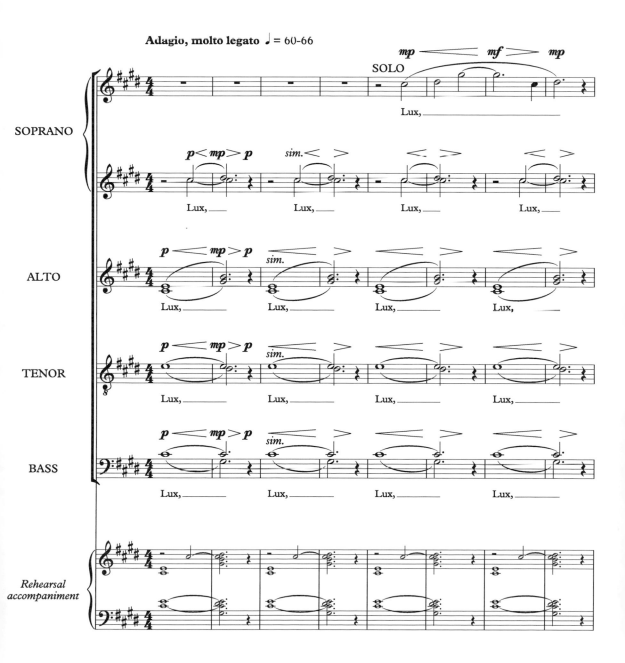

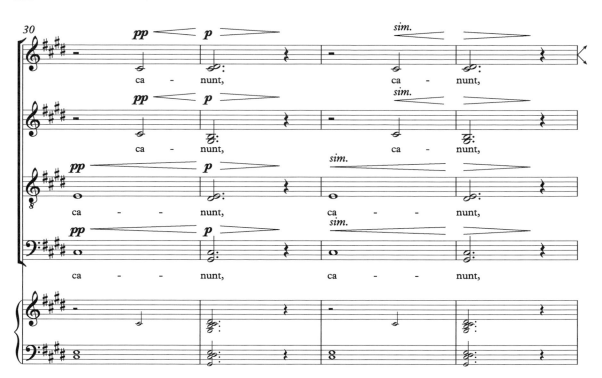

150

O come, all ye faithful

Adeste, fideles

Tr. F. Oakeley,
W.T. Brooke
and others

Words and melody by
J.F. Wade (*c.* 1711-1786)
arranged by David Hill

1. O come, all ye faith - ful, Joy - ful and tri - um - phant, O
2. God of God, Light of Light,

come ye, O come ye to Beth - le - hem;
Lo! he ab - hors not the Vir - gin's womb;

Come and be - hold him Born the King of An - gels: O
Ve - ry God, Be - got - ten, not cre - a - ted:

Man.

come, let us a - dore him, O come, let us a - dore him, O

Ped.

come, let us a - dore him, Christ the Lord:

Note: Verses 1-5 may be sung in unison or harmony as desired.
Verse 6 can be sung with solo descant, with SATB descant, or with both together.

151

3. See how the shepherds,
   Summoned to his cradle,
Leaving their flocks, draw nigh with lowly fear;
   We too will thither
   Bend our joyful footsteps:
     O come, etc.

4. Lo! star-led chieftains,
   Magi, Christ adoring,
Offer him incense, gold, and myrrh;
   We to the Christ Child
   Bring our hearts' oblations:
     O come, etc.

5. Child, for us sinners
   Poor and in the manger,
Fain we embrace thee, with awe and love;
   Who would not love thee,
   Loving us so dearly?
     O come, etc.

152

O come, O come, Emmanuel!

VENI EMMANUEL

Traditional
arr. David Hill

2. O come, thou Wisdom from on high!
   Who madest all in earth and sky,
   Creating man from dust and clay:
   To us reveal salvation's way.

3. O come, O come, Adonaï,
   Who in thy glorious majesty
   From Sinai's mountain, clothed with awe,
   Gavest thy folk the ancient law.

4. O come, thou Root of Jesse! draw
   The quarry from the lion's claw;
   From those dread caverns of the grave,
   From nether hell, thy people save.

5. O come, thou Lord of David's Key!
   The royal door fling wide and free;
   Safeguard for us the heav'nward road,
   And bar the way to death's abode.

6. O come, O come, thou Dayspring bright!
   Pour on our souls thy healing light;
   Dispel the long night's ling'ring gloom,
   And pierce the shadows of the tomb.

7. O come, Desire of nations! show
   Thy kingly reign on earth below;
   Thou Cornerstone, uniting all,
   Restore the ruin of our fall.

from the face of God's___ dear Son. Re - joice! Re - joice! Em -

from the face of God's___ dear Son. Re - joice! Re - joice! Em -

- man - u - el shall come, O Is - ra - el.

- man - u - el shall come to thee, O Is - ra - el.

(Tuba)

O Jesulein süß

O little one sweet

English translation
by Percy Dearmer

German tune
harmonized by J.S. Bach

2. O Jesulein süß, O Jesulein mild,
   Mit Freuden hast du die Welt erfüllt.
      Du kommst herab vons Himmels Saal,
      Und tröstest und in dem Jammertal,
   O Jesulein süß, O Jesulein mild.

3. O Jesulein süß, O Jesulein mild,
   Du bist der Lieb ein Webenbild;
      Zünd an in uns der Liebe Flamm,
      Dass wir dich lieben allzusamm,
   O Jesulein süß, O Jesulein mild.

4. O Jesulein süß, O Jesulein mild,
   Hilf, dass wir tun alls, was du willt;
      Was unser ist, ist alles dein,
      Ach lass uns dir befohlen sein,
   O Jesulein süß, O Jesulein mild.

2. *O little one sweet, O little one mild,*
   With joy thou hast the whole world filled;
      Thou camest here from heav'n's domain,
      To bring men comfort in their pain,
   O little one sweet, O little one mild.

3. *O little one sweet, O little one mild,*
   In thee Love's beauties are all distilled;
      Then light in us thy love's bright flame,
      That we may give thee back the same,
   O little one sweet, O little one mild.

4. *O little one sweet, O little one mild,*
   Help us to do as thou hast willed.
      Lo, all we have belongs to thee!
      Ah, keep us in our fealty!
   O little one sweet, O little one mild.

Of a Rose

Words anon. 14th century

Cecilia McDowall

Pronunciation: yonge as in wrong, non as in known

*aungel with a soft 'g' and long 'au'

translation: tour = tower

*gret as in *yet, seyde* as in *rain/rein*   *flour* as in *floor/poor, breke* as in *let/yet*

heye as in *hay, schen* as in *shen/hen*

tr. *schen* = shining, *heye* = high

*hevene as in heaven, here as in hair

★ *sterre* as in *stair* (meaning 'star')

* *brod* as *brohd*, as in *sew/sow*

* *doun* as *doon*, *blyss'd* as *blist* or *blisd*

tr. swote = sweet

* *schewit* as *shoot*

tr. bote = salvation, schewit = is shown, prystes hond = priest's hand

To the Marchioness of Aberdeen

Puer Nobis

Alice Meynell

Richard Rodney Bennett

Once in royal David's city

C. F. Alexander

H. J. Gauntlett
Harmonized by A. H. Mann
Verses 3 & 6 arranged
by James O'Donnell

Verse 4:
For he is our childhood's pattern,
Day by day like us he grew,
He was little, weak, and helpless,
Tears and smiles like us he knew:
And he feeleth for our sadness,
And he shareth in our gladness.

Verse 5:
And our eyes at last shall see him,
Through his own redeeming love,
For that child so dear and gentle
Is our Lord in heaven above;
And he leads his children on
To the place where he is gone.

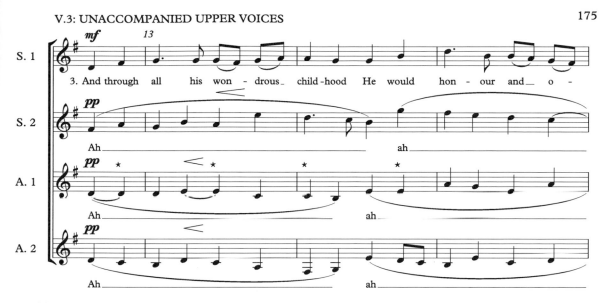

★ The repeated notes should be slightly articulated.

v.6 overleaf

176

Riu, riu, chiu

Juan del Encina (1468-1530)

Mateo Flecha the elder? (1481-1553)
(Villancicos de diversos autores, 1556)

The guarding shepherd by the river: God protected the ewe from the wolf.

Performance note: Perform varying dynamics, instruments and combinations of voices between verses and refrains.

178

1. *The angry wolf tried to attack her, but almighty God protected her:*
   He created her so that she knew no sin and was a virgin unstained by Adam's fault.

2. *This newborn child is the Christ in flesh;*
   He redeemed us by appearing small: he who was infinite became finite.

3. *The prophesies told of his coming and now we see them fulfilled.*
   God became man, we witness him on earth, and we see man in heaven because God loved him.

4. *I saw a thousand angels singing as they flew, making a thousand sounds,*
   Chanting to the Basques 'Glory be in heaven and peace on earth now that Jesus is born!'

5. *He comes to give life to the dead and atone for mankind's sins: this child is the light of day, the Lamb of whom St John spoke.*

6. *Awake! Everybody: God made Mary a mother;*
   He who was her father was born of her today; and he who created her calls herself her son.

4. *Now we have the glorious gift, let us go together to present to him our gifts;*
   Let us to present him our gifts; let each present themselves to God who was willing to come down to earth to become man's equal.

Resonet in laudibus

Michael Praetorius
edited by David Hiley

ge - nu - it__ Ma - ri - a, Sunt im-ple - ta quae prae - dix - it Ga - bri - el.

ge - nu - it Ma - ri - a, Sunt__ im-ple - ta quae prae - dix - it Ga - bri - el.__

ge - nu - it__ Ma - ri - a, Sunt__ im-ple - ta quae prae - dix - it Ga - bri - el.

ge - nu - it__ Ma - ri - a, Sunt im-ple - ta quae prae - dix - it Ga - bri - el.

E - ja, e - ja, Vir - go De - um ge - nu - it, Quem di - vi - na

E - ja, e - ja, Vir - go De - um ge - nu - it, Quem di - vi - na

E - ja, e - ja, Vir - go De - um ge - nu - it, Quem di - vi - na

E - ja, e - ja, Vir - go De - um ge - nu - it, Quem di - vi - na

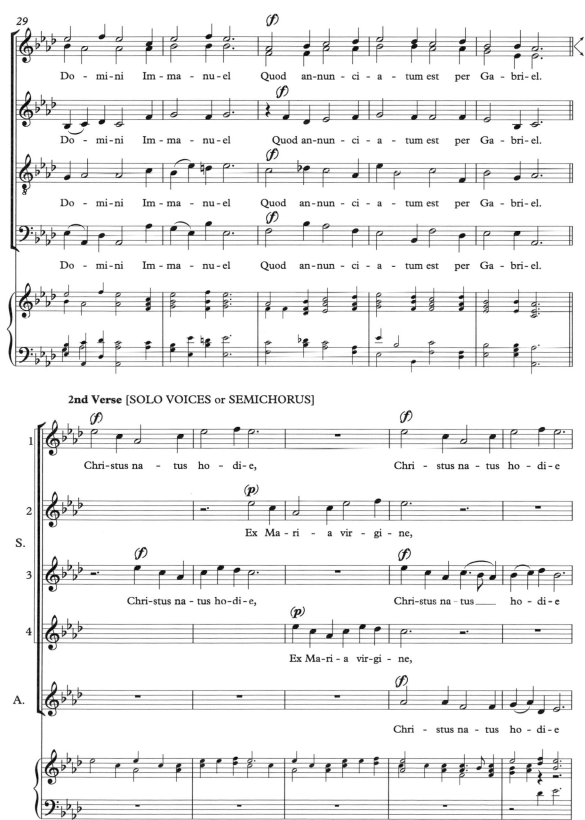

2nd Verse [SOLO VOICES or SEMICHORUS]

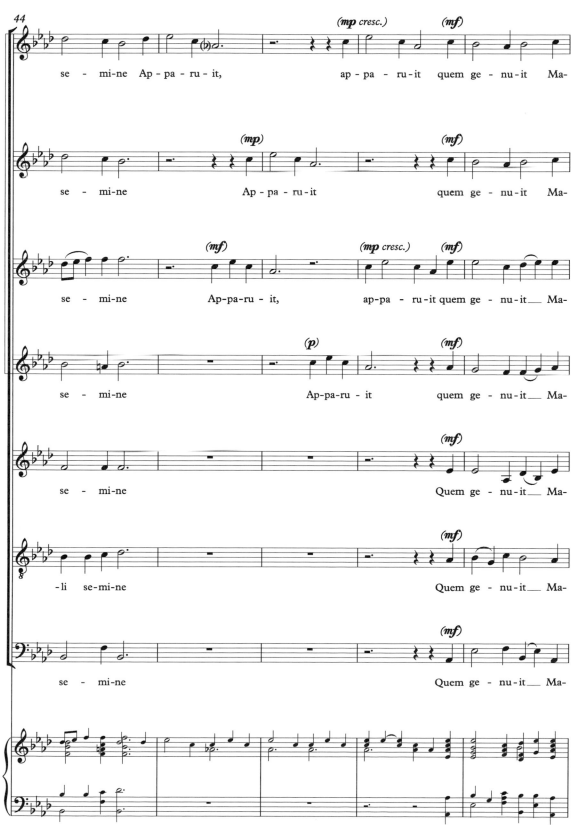

186

188

3rd Verse [TUTTI]

De - o laus et glo - ri - a, Vir - tus est vic - to - ri - a,

Per - pe - te me - mo - ri - a, Ap - pa - ru - it, ap - pa - ru - it Quem

ge - nu - it___ Ma - ri - a. Sunt im-ple - ta quae prae-dix - it

ge - nu - it Ma - ri - a. Sunt___ im-ple - ta quae prae-dix - it

ge - nu - it___ Ma - ri - a. Sunt___ im-ple - ta quae prae - dix - it

ge - nu - it___ Ma - ri - a. Sunt im-ple - ta quae prae-dix - it

Ga - bri - el. E - ja, e - ja, Vir - go De - um

Ga - bri - el.___ E - ja, e - ja, Vir - go De - um

Ga - bri - el. E - ja, e - ja, Vir - go De - um

Ga - bri - el. E - ja, e - ja, Vir - go De - um

ge - nu - it, Quem di - vi - na vo - lu - it cle - men - ti - a.

ge - nu - it, Quem di - vi - na vo - lu - it cle - men - ti - a.

ge - nu - it, Quem di - vi - na vo - lu - it cle - men - ti - a.

ge - nu - it, Quem di - vi - na vo - lu - it cle - men - ti - a.

Ho - di - e ap - pa - ru - it, ap - pa - ru - it in Is - ra - el,

Ho - di - e ap - pa - ru - it, ap - pa - ru - it in Is - ra - el,

Ho - di - e ap - pa - ru - it, ap - pa - ru - it in Is - ra - el,

Ho - di - e ap - pa - ru - it, ap - pa - ru - it in Is - ra - el,

Rocking

John Tavener

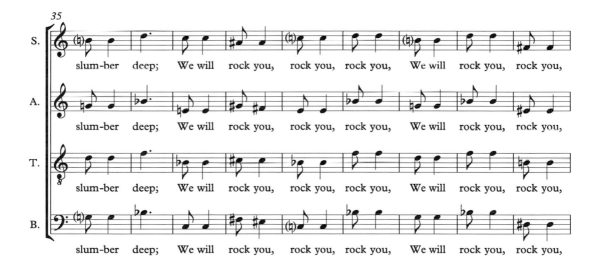

For Herbert and Daisy Powell

St. Joseph's Carol

Traditional Flemish
translated by Elizabeth Poston

Traditional Flemish melody
included by Ernest Closson in his
Chansons populaires des provinces belges, Brussels 1905
arr. Richard Lloyd

Gentle and well sustained ♩ = c.76

1. O see a young maid mo - ther ly - ing, Full of grace and great - ly blest; Hear what gift to her is gi - ven, 'Tis a son, by God's be - hest. Je - sus, Child of Na - za - reth, Be - fore us bit - ter - ly lies cry - ing, Hush, O hush, thou lit - tle babe, hush, God has willed thou li - est here thus.

2. Saint Jo - seph near, in awe be - hold - ing, Rev' - rent -ly holds hat in hand, By the bles - sed Vir - gin Mo - ther There, so thought - ful, he doth stand. In the world a - round him wend - ing, sees he folk of grief un - end - ing,

Man.

Ped.

A.T.B. hum (senza org.)

poco

Performance note: Verse 1 should be sung by a group of three or four Sopranos
Verse 2 Tenor or Baritone solo

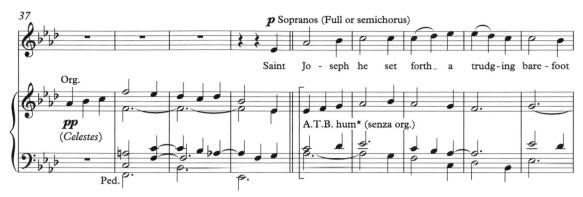

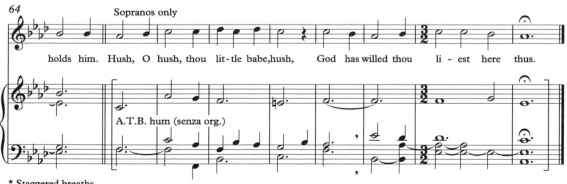

* Staggered breaths.

To the Gentlemen of St John's College, Cambridge

Silent night

Joseph Mohr

Franz Gruber
arr. by David Hill

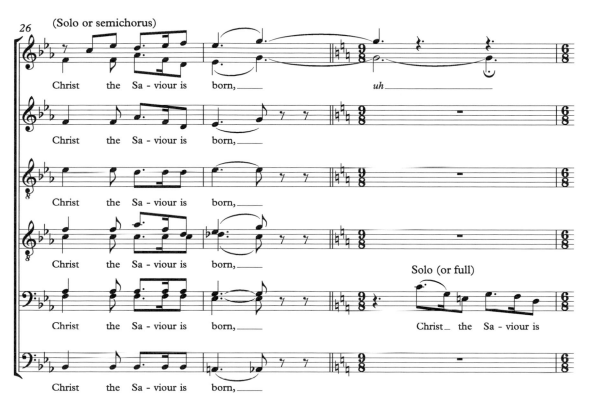

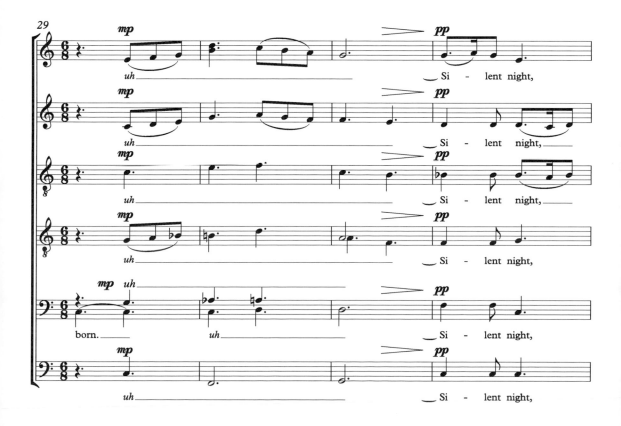

ho - ly night, Son of God, love's pure light,

Solo (or full)

Ra - diant beams— thy ho - ly face With the dawn of re - deem - ing grace.

poco rit.

The Swallow and the Bells

Carol Barratt
Based on a traditional Ukrainian folk chant

Mykola Leontovich (1877-1921)

This have I done for my true love

Old Cornish Poem

Gustav Holst (1874-1934)

214

af-ter-wards bap-tised I was, The Ho-ly Ghost on me did glance, My

af-ter-wards bap-tised I was, The Ho-ly Ghost on me did glance, My

af-ter-wards bap-tised I was, The Ho-ly Ghost on me did glance, My

af-ter-wards bap-tised I was, The Ho-ly Ghost on me did glance, My

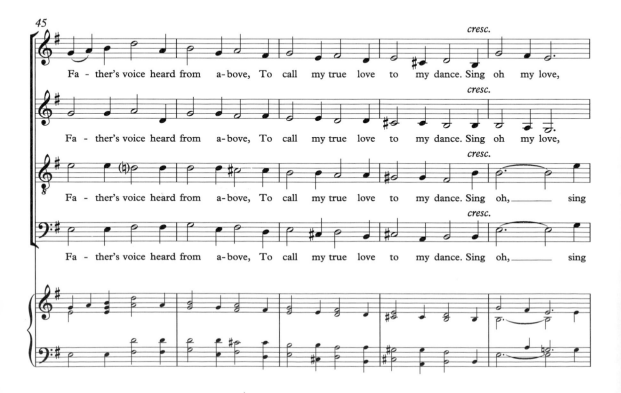

Fa-ther's voice heard from a-bove, To call my true love to my dance. Sing oh my love,

Fa-ther's voice heard from a-bove, To call my true love to my dance. Sing oh my love,

Fa-ther's voice heard from a-bove, To call my true love to my dance. Sing oh, sing

Fa-ther's voice heard from a-bove, To call my true love to my dance. Sing oh, sing

Oh my love, my love, my love. This have I done for my true love.

Oh my love, my love, my love. This have I done for my true love.

oh my love, my love. This have I done for my true love.

oh my love, my love, my love. This have I done for my true love.

In - to the des - ert I was led, Where I fast - ed with - out sub - stance: The

In - to the des - ert I was led, Where I fast - ed with - out sub - stance: The

In - to the des - ert I was led, Where I fast - ed with - out sub - stance: The

In - to the des - ert I was led, Where I fast - ed with - out sub - stance: The

my true love.

my true love.

The Jews on me they made great suit, And with me made great

my true love.

Be - cause they loved dark - ness bet - ter than light, To call my true love

va - ri - ance, Be - cause they love dark - ness bet - ter than light, To call my true love

Be - cause they love dark - ness bet - ter than light, To call my true love

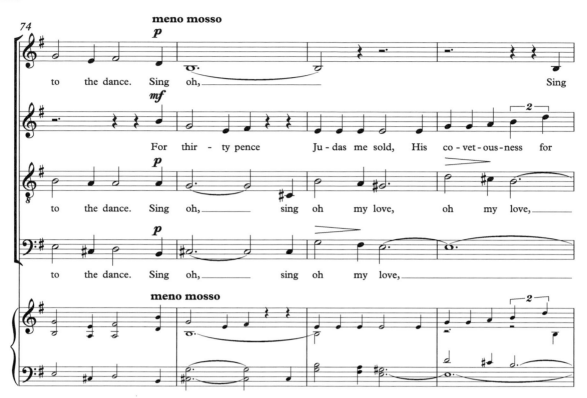

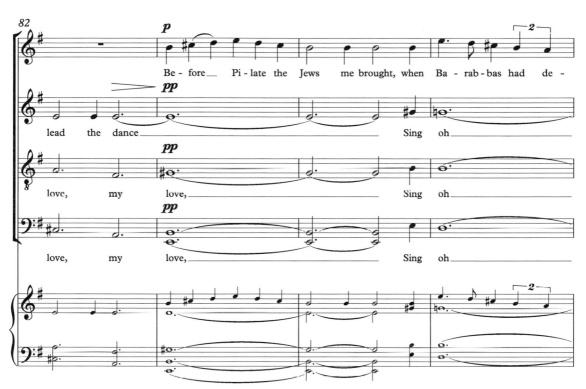

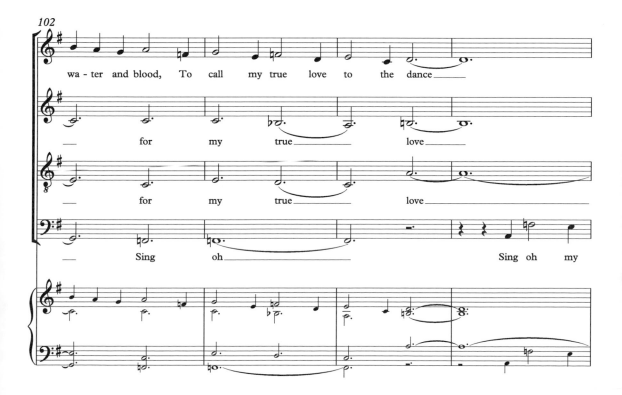

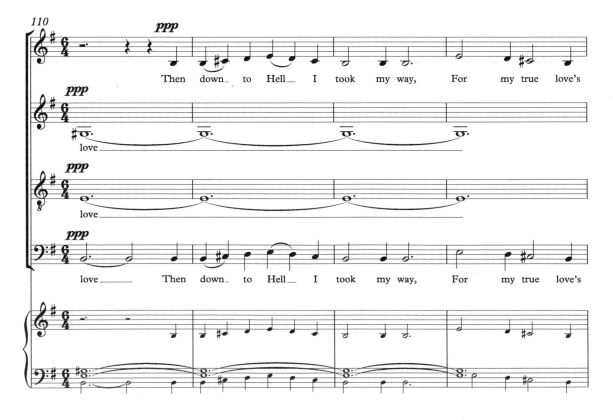

for David Hill and the Choir of St John's College, Cambridge

Threshold of Night

Kathleen Raine
(1908 - 2003)

Tarik O'Regan

234

235

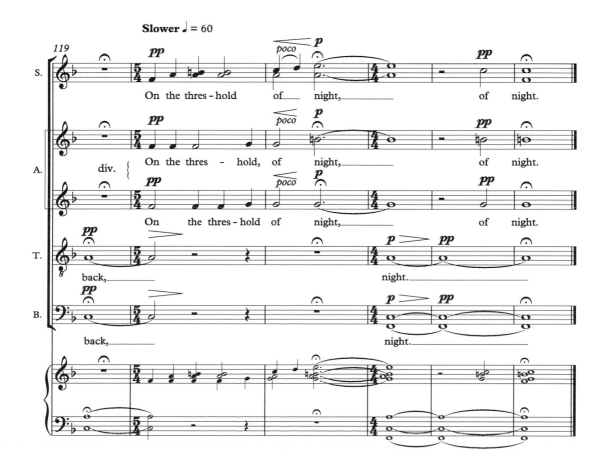

Torches

Translated by J.B. Trend (1887-1958)
from 'The Oxford Book of Carols'

John Joubert

242

Übers Gebirg Maria geht

Johannes Eccard (1553-1611)

1. *Mary walks across the mountains to Elizabeth, her cousin.*
2. *Why are we always staying at home?*

(1.) She greets her friend who, moved by the spirit, praises Mary,
(2.) Let us also go to the mountains to speak to others,

246

(1.) and calls her the Mother of the Lord. Mary became joyful and sang:
(2.) the Spirit makes the heart joyful and excited and the mouth sing in faith:

My soul magnifies the Lord, and my spirit rejoices in God. He is my Saviour, and to be feared.

248

He shall always be merciful.

Venite, Gaudete!

Adrian Peacock

260

For Adrian Lucas and the Choir of Worcester Cathedral

While shepherds watched their flocks by night

Nahum Tate

Ian Venables

270

273

For the Bach Choir

What sweeter music

Robert Herrick
(1591-1674)

Richard Allain

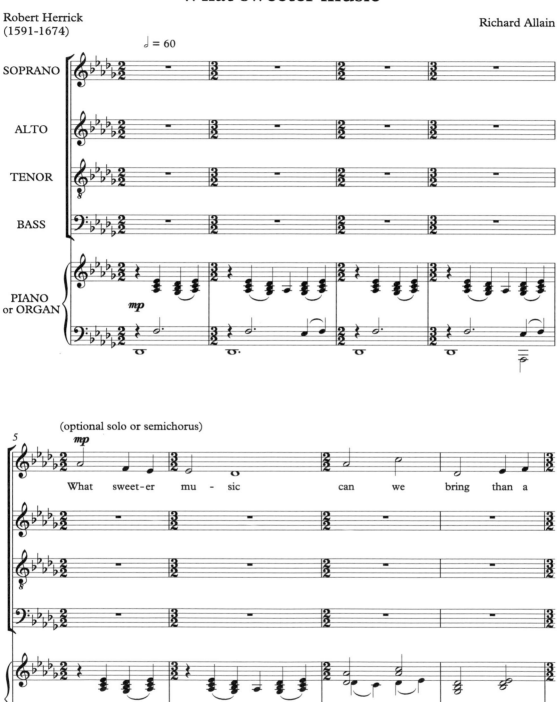

(optional solo or semichorus)

What sweet-er mu - sic can we bring than a

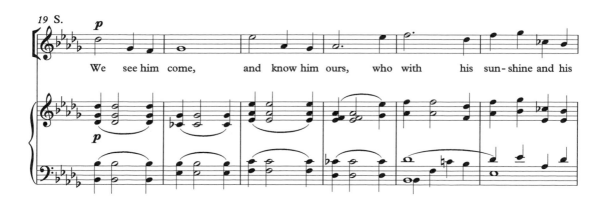

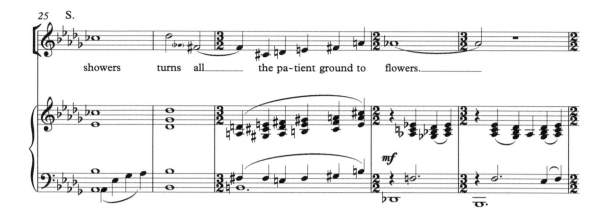

showers turns all_____ the pa-tient ground to flowers._____

Dark and dull night fly hence a-

Dark and dull night fly hence a-

Dark and dull night fly hence a-

Dark and dull night fly hence a-

We see him come, and know him ours, who with his

We see him come, and know him ours, his

We see him come, and know him ours, who with his

We see him come, with

sun-shine and his showers turns all the pa-tient ground to

sun-shine and his showers turns all the pat-ient ground to

sun-shine and his showers turns all the pa-tient ground to

his sun shine and his showers turns,

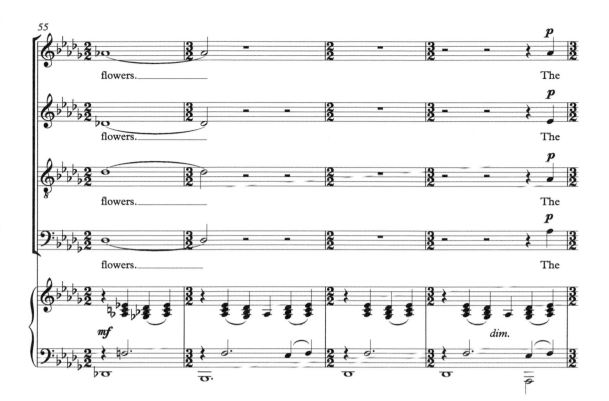

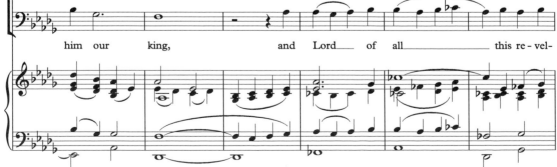

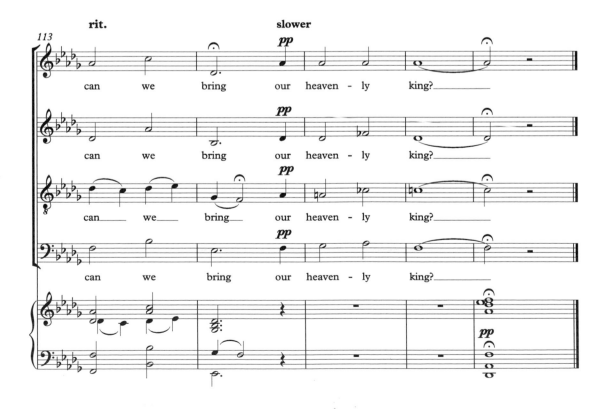

'O' Antiphons
Antiphonarii Cisterciensis

c. 9th century
transcribed by David Hill

'O Sapientia' (December 17th)

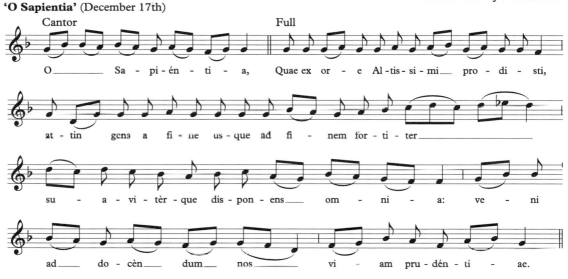

O Wisdom, proceeding from the mouth of the of the Most High, Stretching from end to end,
Disposing all things in strength and sweetness; Come and teach us the way of understanding.

O Sapienta would have been intoned by the 'Lord Abbot from his stall' on December 17th*.

'O Adonai' (December 18th)

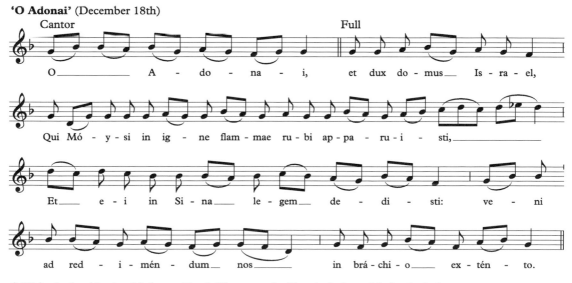

O Mighty Lord and Leader of the house of Israel, Who appeared to Moses in the flame of the burning bush
And gave him the law on Mount Sinai; Come to redeem us with your outstretched arm.

O Adonai would have been intoned by the Prior on December 18th.

* Research by the distinguished scholar Dr Mary Berry into the manuscript of The Ordinale of
St Mary's Abbey, York, shows how the antiphons, dating from the ninth century or earlier, were perfomed
by different members of the Abbey community, with the Precentor assigning who should sing them.

'O Radix Jesse' (December 19th)

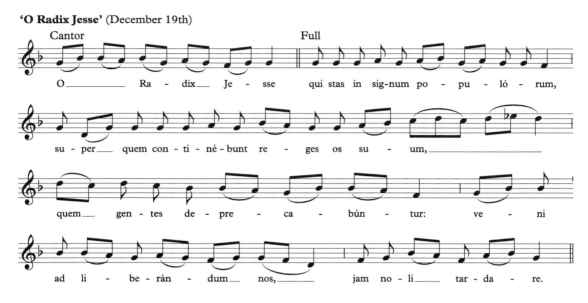

O Root of Jesse, you who stand as a sign for the people, Over whom kings hold their tongue,
Whom the nations implore: Come to free us, do not now delay.

O Radix Jesse would have been intoned by the Almoner on December 19th.

'O Clavis David' (December 20th)

O Key of David, and sceptre of the house of Israel; What you open none can close,
And what you close none can open; Come and lead out to freedom the one
Who is bound in prison, Sitting in darkness and in the shadow of death.

O Clavis David would have been intoned by the Cellarer (the monk with the key to the wine cellar) on December 20th.

'O Oriens' (December 21st)

O Star of the morning, splendour of eternal light, And sun of righteousness:
Come and shine upon those who sit in darkness and in the shadow of death.

O Oriens would have been intoned by the Chamberlain (the monk in charge of the household) on December 21st.

'O Rex Gentium' (December 22nd)

O King of all nations, their desire and the keystone that holds everything together:
Come and redeem mankind whom you fashioned out of clay.

O Rex Gentium would have been intoned by the Plumber on December 22nd.

'O Emmanuel' (December 23rd)

O Emmanuel, our King and lawgiver,
Whom the nations all await as their Saviour;
Come and save us, O Lord our God.

O Emmanuel would have been intoned by the Bursar on December 23rd.

'Hodie' (December 24th and 25th)

Today Christ is born, Today the Saviour has appeared,
Today on earth the angels sing, and archangels rejoice saying:
Glory to God in the highest, Alleluia.

Hodie would have been intoned on 24th and 25th December by the Lord Abbot, as on December 17th.